Social-Emotional Learning for Autistic Kids

Social-Emotional Learning for Autistic Kids

Fun Activities to Manage Big Feelings and Make Friends

Emily Mori, MS, LCPC, CAS

Illustrated by Victoria Stebleva

Z Kids • New York

Published in the United States by Z Kids, an imprint of Zeitgeist™, a division of Penguin Random House LLC, New York.
zeitgeistpublishing.com

Zeitgeist™ is a trademark of Penguin Random House LLC
ISBN: 9780593690444

Illustrations by Victoria Stebleva
Book design by Aimee Fleck and Emma Hall
Author photograph © by Jeff Benzon
Edited by Ada Fung

Printed in the United States of America
1st Printing

Thank you, Mom, Dad, Katie, Chris, and
Luke, for your continued support.
Thank you, Eric, for always being my inspiration.

Contents

• •

CHAPTER 1:

Be Your True You 17

CHAPTER 2:

Big Feelings and How to Handle Them 33

Introduction for Parents and Caregivers

I imagine you picked up this book because you are concerned about your child making friends. Perhaps your child has shared with you that they often feel misunderstood by the kids (and grown-ups!) in their life. Maybe you worry that no one will come to their birthday party or sit with them at lunch at school. I've met a lot of kids and parents who are in the same boat—that's why I decided to write this book! Helping autistic kids has been a longtime passion of mine. As a licensed clinical professional counselor, I have seen firsthand how the activities in this book have helped autistic kids feel more confident in the world around them.

The intention of this book is to give kiddos a helping hand as they learn how to navigate social situations, especially those that may feel scary or overwhelming. I've written it from a neurodiversity-affirming perspective, meaning that it does not encourage masking or aim to "fix" your kid. I believe that every child is special and wonderful in their own way. The strengths they possess, as well as the challenges that they experience, make them who they are.

Throughout this book, I use identity-first language (*autistic kids*) and not person-first language (*kids with autism*). This is because autistic people tend to prefer identity-first language, and I hope that by using it here, it will encourage kids to think positively about their condition. However, some autistic people do use person-first language—I find that this choice is quite personal to the individual.

The activities in this book are designed to help kids better identify their feelings, express their emotions, and advocate for themselves.

Most of the book's activities can be individualized for each child's needs and goals. The "Activity Tips" will provide some ideas for how to do so. You can also use the "Activities by Subject" and "Activities by Modality" indexes at the back of the book (pages 155-156) to find specific activities to suit your kid's needs.

Many of the activities can be done independently by the kids. But I've included ways to involve grown-ups in the activities, because I've found that one of the best ways for parents and caregivers to support their child's social-emotional learning is by doing the activities with them and by sharing their own experiences. In addition, the "Caregiver Tips" in the activities will aid you in helping your child expand on the skills they've learned in this book and keep practicing them in their everyday lives.

Finally, it is important to note that while I hope this book will serve as a helpful resource, it is not a substitute for professional advice or treatment. If you feel your child could benefit from additional help, I wholeheartedly encourage you to seek supportive and neurodiversity-affirming care for them.

Introduction for Kids

Welcome to this super-special activity book! I wrote it especially for you because I want you to know how wonderful and unique you are.

I also know that sometimes it's hard for you to express what you're feeling. Maybe you're overwhelmed with all the emotions inside your body. Maybe you find it hard to make friends. Or maybe you find it hard to get people to listen to you and understand you. This book can help you with all of that!

You're going to play games and do activities that will help you figure out your feelings, embrace who you are, express yourself clearly and confidently, and learn how to make friends. You can do these activities alone or, if you want or need help, with a grown-up. I hope you'll like them so much that you'll want to share them with your family and friends.

Before you begin, I want you to know that this book—while super fun—may also be a bit hard and tiring. If it starts to feel that way, be sure to talk to a grown-up you trust, like a parent, counselor, or teacher. They can help you work through your thoughts and feelings and figure out when you need to take a break. Also know that you don't have to do every activity in this book. If there's one that feels too difficult or just not right for you, you can skip it!

I'm so happy you're here. I really hope you enjoy the book!

Why Develop Social-Emotional Learning?

Have you ever heard a grown-up say something like "It's important to feel comfortable in your own skin"? What does that even mean? Well, it's about loving yourself just the way you are. This includes the parts you really like about yourself, such as creating awesome buildings with Legos or being a super-good speller. But it also means learning to handle the times you feel frustrated. Like when your friend doesn't want to play Star Wars the way you want to, or when your parent forgets to wash your favorite pajamas and you don't want to wear anything else to bed.

Being at school is probably a big part of your life, so this book is about helping you feel comfortable around your classmates, whether in class or on the playground. I know that sometimes being with other kids can feel overwhelming or upsetting, like when you're in the schoolyard and everyone is running around playing a game and it all feels like too much. Or when you're waiting for your turn at the library to check out a book only to find someone else got it first.

You might have heard the term *social skills*, and you might even already know that it involves learning how to interact with the world around us, including our friends, family—even strangers. But, as a therapist, I like to think bigger and help kids work on their *social-emotional learning.* The reason I like that term is that it not only includes what's outside (our social life), but also what's inside (our emotions).

That's a lot, right? To help, try thinking of social-emotional learning as a toolbox filled with different skills to help you handle the ups and downs of everyday life. It's learning how to understand and manage your emotions. It's about setting goals and achieving them. It's about learning how to show empathy for others. And it's about developing fulfilling relationships.

I also want you to remember that there's no one right way to make friends or talk about your feelings. Everyone is different, and that's okay! I want you to do things in a way that makes you feel comfortable and confident. And if ever there is a change that you find hard, this book will help you develop coping strategies that will help you navigate those situations.

Everybody works on their social and emotional skills, including your friends, your classmates, and even grown-ups! So, don't be hard on yourself if you don't get it right away. You'll get lots of practice in this book until you feel confident using these skills in your everyday life.

Let's get started!

CHAPTER 1

BE YOUR TRUE YOU

There is only one YOU in the entire world—how amazing is that?!
Even so, I bet there have been times when you didn't feel so special
or awesome. These kinds of feelings happen to all of us. The good
thing is this chapter can help you understand why you feel this way.
More importantly, you will learn how to develop skills so you CAN feel
better about yourself and what you offer the world! In this chapter,
you'll learn how to

- talk about your likes and dislikes
- understand what brings you joy, happiness, and comfort
- be more comfortable about who you are and what makes
  you great
- better understand what makes you feel uncomfortable,
  so you'll know when that feeling begins to creep up in
  your body

All about Me Trading Card

Think about a Pokémon or a baseball card. What do you remember? They are small cards and have a picture of a character or person along with some information about them. That's what you are going to create here, only about yourself! The goal is to help you see what a wonderful and unique person you are.

Directions

1. Draw a picture of yourself in the blank box.
2. Fill in the blanks of your trading card—ask a grown-up if you need help.
3. Share your card with your family, and talk about your answers with them.
4. If you like, you can make copies of the card to share with others.

Activity Tip: Ask family members to create their own cards and play a guessing game! Guess what they wrote, and have them guess what you wrote.

Social-Emotional Learning for Autistic Kids

NAME: _____

BIRTHDAY: _____

FAVORITE ANIMAL: _____

FAVORITE FOOD: _____

I LOVE: _____

I DON'T LIKE: _____

MY SUPER-COOL SKILL IS: _____

I WANT TO LEARN: _____

Superhero Showdown!

Sometimes our worries and fears can feel so big, they seem like monsters. But you have the superpowers within you to quiet those scary feelings! The trick is to say positive words to yourself about yourself. In this activity, you're going to write things you like about yourself on a drawing of a superhero cape. The next time you're scared or worried, throw on your imaginary cape!

What You Need

- Colored pencils or markers (optional)

- Stickers (optional)

Directions

1. Think about what you like about yourself. Try to come up with 3 to 5 different things.
2. Inside the superhero cape, write positive "I" statements that describe your strengths. See the examples around the drawing for inspiration!
3. Decorate the cape with drawings or stickers, if you like.
4. Practice saying your "I" statements out loud so you can remember them whenever you feel scared, worried, or need a little boost.

Activity Tip: Create a real superhero cape with fabric, and use fabric markers to write your positive "I" statements.

I am strong

I am kind

I am creative

I can do hard things

BE YOUR TRUE YOU

Growing a Social Garden

Picture a garden with beautiful flowers. Those flowers started off as small seeds that needed lots of time and care to grow. Social and emotional skills are the same way! The first step is to figure out what social situations make you feel uncomfortable or icky. This activity will help you figure out how to feel more at ease.

Directions

1. Think of 3 social situations that make you feel nervous or uncomfortable. Examples might include recess, small group or partner time, or a big party.
2. At the center of each flower, write one of these social situations.
3. In the petals, write ideas for how you can feel more comfortable in each situation. Ideas might include staying close to a friend, bringing a stuffie, or asking a grown-up for help.

Caregiver Tip: Some autistic kids find it easier to have difficult conversations while doing a sensory activity. Instead of doing this activity on the page, choose a few different plants to grow with your kid. As you work together to plant the seeds, talk about what your child needs to help them grow and flourish, just like the plants.

My Time Capsule

When I was little, I really loved pink bubble-gum ice cream. Now chocolate is my favorite. It is totally natural for our likes and dislikes to change over time. What's fun is to see how your interests have changed, because it helps you understand how much you've grown as a person!

What You Need

- A shoebox
- Art supplies (markers, paint, stickers)

Directions

1. Decorate the shoebox using your art supplies.
2. Write a letter to yourself about things that make you feel happy, like favorite hobbies or favorite people to spend time with. Include your hopes for the future, like what you want to do when you grow up or a skill you hope to learn. Ask a grown-up to help with writing if needed.
3. Draw a picture of how you imagine your future self will look.
4. Add your letter, picture, and the other items on the Time Capsule Checklist to your box.
5. With the help of a grown-up, put your time capsule in a special place you can visit later.

Time Capsule Checklist

☐ A drawing of your favorite stuffed animal or other comfort item

☐ A picture of your favorite food or a (clean) wrapper from a favorite snack

☐ Something that represents a favorite hobby (but not something you'll miss!)

☐ A picture of yourself at your current age

Get to Know Me Scavenger Hunt

You know who you are and what you like, but how much do other people know about you? Help the people in your life get to know you better by finding items that represent who you are and sharing them.

Directions

1. Search through your home to find the items on the checklist.
2. Gather your family and friends, and share with them your items and why you chose them.

Caregiver Tip: Take the pressure off your kid by making this a family activity! Divvy up the prompts between those participating, and ask everyone to share their items.

Social-Emotional Learning for Autistic Kids

Scavenger Hunt Checklist

☐ Something that brings you comfort

☐ Something you are proud of

☐ Something you dislike

☐ Something you do for fun

☐ Something that reminds you of home

☐ Something that reminds you of a friend or family member

Soundtrack of My Life

Music is awesome. It's fun to dance to, and it can make you feel good! Songs help us express who we are and connect us to what we feel at a moment in time. Create a soundtrack for yourself by putting together a list of songs for different moments in your life.

Directions

1. Using the prompts, write down the name of a song that feels right for each moment or feeling. These should be songs you know and like.
2. With permission from a grown-up, use the Internet to listen to the songs as you create your soundtrack.
3. Keep this list of songs somewhere you can see so you remember to put the song on whenever the need strikes!

Caregiver Tip: For children who don't like music or experience sound sensitivity, consider what is important to them. Is it sports, books, art? Help your child identify what they enjoy that provides them encouragement and comfort when confronting big scenarios and feelings!

AT THE BEGINNING OF THE DAY:

WHEN I WANT TO DANCE AND WIGGLE:

WHEN I'M ABOUT TO DO SOMETHING NEW:

AT THE END OF THE DAY:

WHEN I'M SCARED:

Chapter Wrap-Up

Hooray, you finished the first chapter! Let's review. You learned about how it's important to make sure to be true to yourself even if it can sometimes feel easier to change to fit in. That's because the more comfortable you are in your own skin, the more you'll be able to confidently express your needs, feelings, and ideas! Remember to:

- Focus on the things that bring you comfort and joy just like you did in the **Get to Know Me Scavenger Hunt** (page 26).
- Re-read your **All about Me Trading Card** (page 18) when you need a reminder about how wonderful you are.
- When you are feeling nervous or anxious, put on your imaginary cape from **Superhero Showdown!** (page 20).
- Put on the songs from your **Soundtrack of My Life** (page 28) to help you feel better.

Social-Emotional Learning for Autistic Kids

CHAPTER 2

BIG FEELINGS AND HOW TO HANDLE THEM

The feelings you have going on in your body and mind are usually different every day, sometimes every hour. It depends on what's happening around you and inside you. You might wake up happy and excited, then feel sad and angry by recess, and then happy again at lunch. Sometimes, your emotions might feel so big that they feel like they might just bubble up and explode out of your body like a soda bottle that has been shaken up. In this chapter, you'll do activities that will help you learn to handle your big feelings, like learning how to

- identify and understand the emotions that you feel
- take big, deep breaths and use other coping skills to help you calm down when you're feeling overwhelmed
- express how you feel in a way that makes sense to you and the people around you
- understand the body language and emotions of other kids and people around you

Be sure to practice these activities so you can start to feel more in control when difficult moments happen to you.

Feelings Wheel

Explaining how we feel in times of extreme happiness, sadness, and anger isn't always easy. Sometimes our emotions are so big, it's hard to find the right words. In this activity, you will create a feelings wheel and practice using it to communicate how you feel.

What You Need

- A grown-up
- Pencil
- Ruler
- Paper plate
- Colored pencils or markers
- Stickers (optional)
- Clothespin

Directions

1. Read the list of feelings words on page 35. Talk with a grown-up about what they mean.
2. Use a pencil and a ruler to divide your plate into six equal sections, like the picture on page 36.
3. Write a feelings word in each section. Pick ones that you feel most often.
4. Color each section a different color, based on the emotion. For example, you might use yellow for happy or blue for sad.
5. Add drawings or stickers that describe each feeling.
6. Next, on the clothespin, use a marker to write the words "I feel."
7. Practice using the wheel with your parents or another family member by moving the clothespin to the emotion you're feeling at any time. For example, you could use it when you get home from school to discuss how your day went.

Feelings Words

- Happy
- Sad
- Angry
- Annoyed
- Frustrated
- Scared

- Worried
- Excited
- Confused
- Confident
- Shy

CONTINUED →

Caregiver Tip: Help your child practice by modeling using their feelings wheel to share your feelings with them.

Social-Emotional Learning for Autistic Kids

Five Senses Brain Break

Isn't it amazing that our bodies can see, smell, hear, touch, and taste? Together, these are called your five senses. When you're feeling over-whelmed, worried, or scared, it can help to practice using these five senses to calm down. But you don't need to use all five senses if that doesn't feel good for you. For example, if you're sensitive to noise, skip that and just focus on what you can see or touch!

Directions

1. Take 3 deep breaths in and out to ground yourself.
2. Walk around your house and use your senses to fill in the activity.

Caregiver Tip: Take your child on a sensory walk. Take turns pointing out what you see, touch, hear, smell, and taste along the way.

CONTINUED ➔

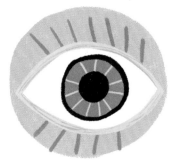

5 THINGS
YOU CAN SEE:

_____

_____

_____

_____

_____

4 THINGS
YOU CAN TOUCH:

_____

_____

_____

_____

**3 THINGS
YOU CAN HEAR:**

_____

_____

_____

**2 THINGS
YOU CAN SMELL:**

_____

_____

**1 THING
YOU CAN TASTE:**

_____

Square Breathing

When you experience a scary, worrisome, or even exciting event, your body immediately reacts. Your heart rate speeds up, your body feels tingly, and your breathing becomes quick and fast. In this exercise, you're going to learn a special breathing pattern to help you calm your body down whenever you feel scared or worried.

Directions

1. Place your pointer finger on the yellow star at the bottom of the square to begin.
2. Move your finger up the side of the square while breathing in for 4 seconds. Stop at the top corner.
3. Move your finger along the top of the square while holding your breath for 4 seconds.
4. Move your finger down the side of the square while breathing out for 4 seconds. Stop at the bottom corner.
5. Move your finger along the bottom of the square while resting for 4 seconds.
6. Repeat 3 to 5 more times. Now practice this breathing pattern while you draw the square in the air.

Caregiver Tip: Incorporate this as part of your bedtime routine together. It will help mindful breathing become a go-to coping skill for them.

Coping Skills Toolbox

As you just learned, putting your five senses to use is a great way to help you feel calm. In this activity, you'll create a toolbox of items—like a piece of chewelry, a fidget toy, or a special stuffie—that you can hold, chew, smell, or look at to make you feel less worried.

What You Need

- Cardboard box of any size
- Colored pencils or markers
- Wrapping paper (optional)
- Scissors (optional)
- Tape (optional)

Directions

1. Decorate the box you've chosen for your coping skills toolbox. Color it, draw on it, or cover it in fun wrapping paper!
2. Fill the box with your comfort items. Use the list of suggestions on page 43 to help.
3. Use the items in the box whenever you feel sad, scared, mad, or worried. You can always take an item from it with you if you think you'll be going somewhere that might cause anxiety or be overstimulating.

Caregiver Tip: If your child is overwhelmed by choices, give them 2 items out of each category to pick from.

Comfort Item Suggestions

- Something that reminds me of home

- Something that smells nice

- A favorite fidget toy

- Something cozy or warm

- A favorite photo or drawing

Feelings Thermometer

When you're feeling sick, a thermometer can tell you if you have a fever. In this activity, you'll use a thermometer to understand your own emotions and figure out how you might bring down a super-hot feelings temperature. One important thing: It's best to first practice this when you're feeling calm so you get the hang of it.

Directions

1. Think about a time when you have felt each of the emotions on the thermometer and how your body responded. For example, how does your body feel when you are calm? What about when you're angry? Does your face feel hot or does your body feel tense?
2. Write down your body signals for each emotion on the side of the thermometer.
3. When you start feeling frustrated, look at your thermometer. Use it to notice how your body is feeling so you can sort through your feelings as they come up.

Caregiver Tip: Make a copy of the thermometer, and tape it to a wall or on the refrigerator so your child can easily see it. Prompt them to use the thermometer as a visual aid to talk about their feelings.

I'm feeling . . .

Body Signals

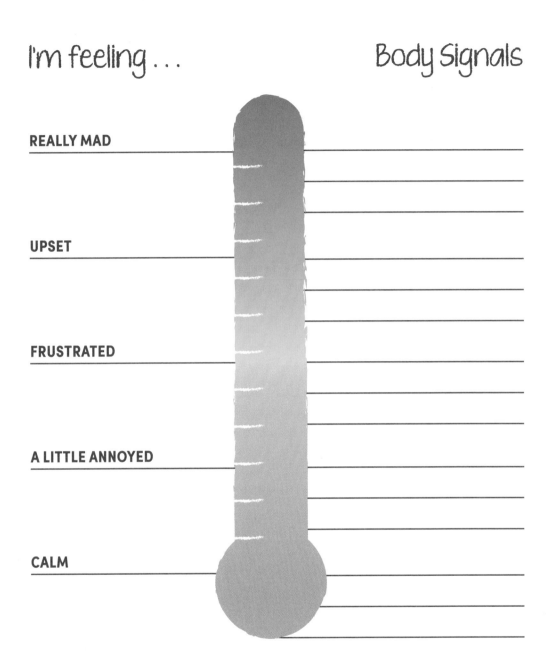

REALLY MAD

UPSET

FRUSTRATED

A LITTLE ANNOYED

CALM

Play Dough Faces

We make different facial expressions every day—it's how we show what we're feeling and thinking. For example, if something is funny or we are happy, we might have a smile on our face. Facial expressions also tell us about how other people feel and/or what they are thinking. What information do you gather when someone frowns at you? Roll and shape the play dough as many times as you want to explore different emotions.

What You Need

- Play dough
- A grown-up

Directions

1. On the blank face, using the play dough, create a facial expression you've seen on someone else. This could be a smile, a frown, or tears.
2. Share with a grown-up what this person might be feeling or thinking.
3. Repeat as many times as you like, creating different facial expressions each time.

Social-Emotional Learning for Autistic Kids

BIG FEELINGS AND HOW TO HANDLE THEM

Chapter Wrap-Up

· ·

In this chapter, you learned about your big feelings: what they mean and how to handle them. You took time to understand the different thoughts that go through your mind and how those thoughts feel in your body. You also learned some cool tricks and tips to help you cope with those feelings. Remember:

- When you feel sad or mad about something, use **Square Breathing** (page 40) to help calm down.
- If you're having difficulty expressing your feelings, you can use your **Feelings Wheel** (page 34) to help.
- Use the items in your **Coping Skills Toolbox** (page 42) to bring you comfort if your big feelings are hard to let go of.

Social-Emotional Learning for Autistic Kids

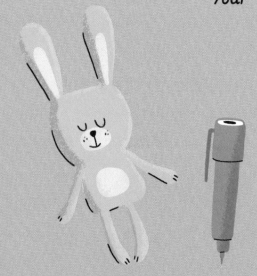

CHAPTER 3

EXPRESS YOURSELF!

It can be hard and scary to stay true to yourself when people—especially grown-ups—tell you to act differently from how you feel or to change how you express yourself. And even when you know exactly how you feel or what you need, you might find it difficult to tell others. When you can express yourself, you are more likely to feel like you have a say in what happens to you. In this chapter, you are going to practice how to

- explore different, creative ways to express yourself
- ask for help and be specific about your needs
- understand what things about yourself you may want to keep to yourself and what you may want to share with others

Learning how to clearly express yourself can also help you make better friends, because when you can tell others what you need, they are more likely to understand and help you. Plus, learning how to express yourself can make you feel braver and stronger!

Express Yourself Story

Writing a story about yourself is a great way to understand your likes and dislikes. I've given you a jump start on your story. All you have to do is fill in the blank spaces! Don't forget to draw a fun picture of yourself!

Directions

1. Fill in the blanks to complete the story so that it describes you.
2. On page 54, draw a picture of yourself in the story.

• •

Hi there,

My name is _____

and I am _____ years old! My birthday is _____.

There are _____ people in my house, and we live in the

city/town of _____

_____.

    My favorite subject in school is _____.

One of my favorite things to do is _____

_____ because _____

_____.

I also like to _____ and _____. My least favorite

thing to do is _____ because

_____.

    When I am feeling _____,

the person who helps me feel better is _____.

When I am feeling sad or mad or angry, I try to cheer

myself up by _____

_____.

    Sometimes, I wish people knew that I'm really good at

_____ and _____.

I find it hard to _____

_____.

I feel nervous when I _____

_____.

    In my class, I'd like to get to know _____

better. I think we could be friends because we both like

_____

_____. CONTINUED →

DRAW HERE:

Social-Emotional Learning for Autistic Kids

Accommodation Station

All trains have conductors. They are responsible for making sure the passengers get to their destination. In this activity, you're going to pretend to be the train conductor of your life. Part of that means learning how to ask for extra help or some changes so that you can feel more comfortable, or better participate in an activity. These are called your accommodations! This activity will help you identify what you need and how to ask for it so you can be in charge of your life.

Directions

1. Using the space in the smoke puffs, write down answers to each prompt on page 56.
2. On page 57, answer the prompt, then draw a picture of yourself as the super-awesome conductor of your life!

Caregiver Tip: Many schools will work with your family to figure out what accommodations your kid may need to help them learn and feel their best. For example, they might give them a special chair to help them sit more comfortably or give them a helper to work with them one-on-one. Make sure your kids know what accommodations are available so they know what they can ask for.

CONTINUED ➔

What I need help with . . .

AT HOME

AT SCHOOL

AT A FRIEND'S HOUSE

Social-Emotional Learning for Autistic Kids

I ask for help when I feel:

_____

_____

_____

DRAW HERE:

Emotion Charades

Charades is a guessing game. It's when someone gives you clues to a word or name by acting out those words or the name. The names you are supposed to guess could be movies, TV shows, or songs. For this exercise, you are going to play charades, but you're going to act out different emotions that you feel in different situations.

What You Need

- Index cards
- Friends and family
- Timer

Directions

1. Write each prompt on an individual index card. Feel free to add your own.
2. Put them facedown in a pile and shuffle them around.
3. Take a card and read what is on the card (in your head!).
4. Set a timer for 2 minutes.
5. Act out the situation on the card. Be sure to use facial expressions and body language!
6. The others will then guess the situation and emotions. If someone hasn't guessed the answer within 2 minutes, reveal the answer.
7. Go around the room until everyone has had a turn!

Activity Tip: You can play this game in a different way by drawing the scenes (make sure to include facial expressions and body language). Then have your friends and family guess what's happening.

- Losing a game

- Failing a test that you studied for

- Forgetting your homework

- Winning a competition

- Celebrating your birthday

- Feeling left out

- A classmate making fun of you

- Being scared of your friend's dog

- Being in trouble for something you didn't do

- Eating in a restaurant that is too loud

"I Am Me" Vision Board

Vision boards are creative ways to show the world all the different things that interest you. You create one by going through magazines and cutting out words and pictures that you think best represent you. These can be pictures of animals, people, movie or book characters, flowers, or favorite colors—really, anything that you find interesting and inspiring!

What You Need

- Magazines
- Scissors
- Piece of cardboard
- Glue

Directions

1. Look through the magazines and find images and words that describe you. Cut them out.
2. Arrange them on the piece of cardboard any way you like and glue them down.

Activity Tip: Get everyone in your family to make vision boards for themselves. When you've finished, have everyone share their creations.

What's Your Hidden Treasure?

Treasure is always very special. In the movies, treasure is usually trunks of gold and jewelry that very few people know about. There are probably some special things about you that only a few people know about or that you've never told anyone before—just like movie treasure! In this activity, think of things that may surprise people who know you. What's your secret treasure?

What You Need

- A grown-up

Directions

1. Answer the prompts along the trail on the treasure map on pages 62-63.
2. Discuss your answers with a trusted grown-up. Why did you keep these things about you a secret?

Caregiver Tip: Use this activity to talk with your child about privacy. Some autistic children have difficulty determining what information they should share and with whom. They may overshare, which can lead to them becoming embarrassed, being taken advantage of, or being bullied.

CONTINUED ➔

Something that scares you
that you've kept secret

Something about you that you think
your friends may not like if they knew

Something your parents
don't know about you
(but you wish they did)

Something that is really
hard for you that others
may not know about

Your Theme Song

Many of us enjoy music and have favorite songs we connect to. Sometimes it's the tune that sticks with us. Other times, it's the words, also called *lyrics*, that make us feel things inside. For this exercise, you're going to write a theme song about yourself. Think of it as a song that describes you on your best day!

Directions

1. Pick a tune that means something special to you. It can be a well-known song such as "Happy Birthday," or maybe you have a favorite song that you listen to a lot right now.
2. Write lyrics that express who you are and what makes you special.
3. Play the song while you are coming up with the lyrics.
4. When you're happy with your theme song lyrics, don't forget to give your song a name!

Activity Tip: Music not your thing? Make a photo mash-up of your favorite things instead! Cut out pictures from magazines, newspapers, or images you find online (be sure to check with a grown-up first).

Name of my theme song:

Chapter Wrap-Up

. . . .

How you see yourself, what you like and dislike, and what you need help with will change as you grow up. But knowing how to express your thoughts and feelings is a skill that will help you all through your life! It can feel funny at times to show your true self if you feel different from the people around you. But the truth is everyone is different! If you ever struggle with expressing yourself, you can try the following:

- Read your **Express Yourself Story** (page 52). Has everything stayed the same, or have some things changed about you? Redo it if things have changed, and use it as a way to practice talking about your likes and dislikes.

- Use "I" statements. Simply saying the words *I feel* or *I need* can help you get started with expressing yourself! Don't forget you can always use your **Feelings Wheel** from Chapter 2 (page 34) to help, too!

- Check in with your inner conductor. Revisit the **Accommodation Station** activity (page 55), and use it to help you communicate your needs when you feel at a loss for words.

CHAPTER 4

BEING SOCIAL

Being social, like having a play date with friends, going to school, or visiting family, can be fun and exciting. It can also be a little bit scary and hard, especially if it's your first time in this type of setting. One way to make social events, situations, and settings not so scary is to understand what you like and don't like about them and why. In this chapter's activities, you will

- think through different social situations, how they make you feel, and how you might act in them
- learn important social-emotional words and ideas
- practice skills that are important for getting along with others, like sharing and respecting other people's opinions

Social Traffic Light

Traffic lights play an important role when it comes to our safety. They let drivers know when to go (green), when to stop (red), and when to slow down (yellow). In this activity, you're going to use a traffic light to figure out how you feel about different social situations.

What You Need

- A grown-up

Directions

1. Think about how the social situations listed below make you feel.
2. Using the emotions key to help you, write down 2 social situations in each circle of the traffic light. Feel free to use or include other social situations.
3. Discuss your traffic light with a grown-up.

Social Situations

- First day of school
- A big birthday party
- A sleepover at a friend's house
- Visiting family in a different state or country
- Playing with my siblings or close friends
- Giving a speech in class

Caregiver Tip: Brainstorm with your child the different ways they can feel better and cope with "yellow" and "red" activities if they are unavoidable.

Emotions Key

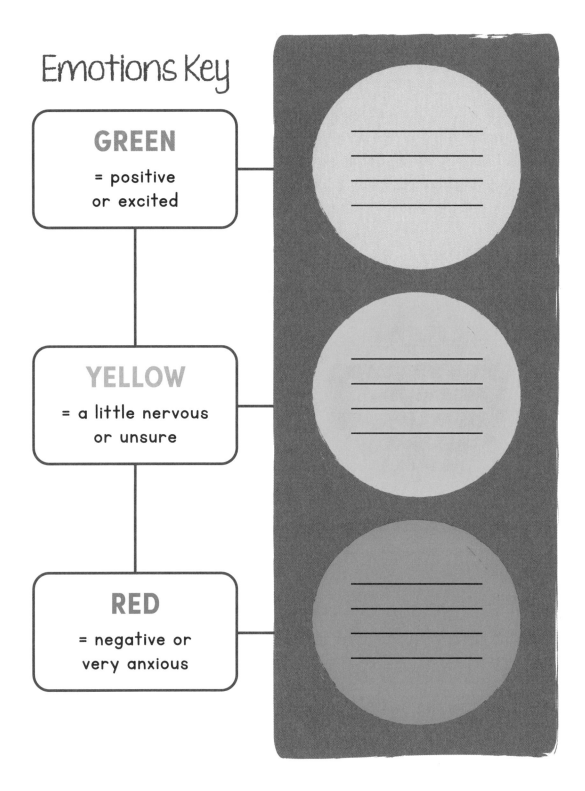

GREEN

= positive
or excited

YELLOW

= a little nervous
or unsure

RED

= negative or
very anxious

Name That Social-Emotional Word!

Let's play a fun game to help you learn and understand important social-emotional words! As you learned in Chapter 2, naming your emotions can help you better express yourself. In much the same way, growing your social-emotional vocabulary can help you better understand what helps (or doesn't help) us all get along.

What You Need

- Friends and family
- Index cards

Directions

1. Write each word on an individual index card. Place the cards facedown in a stack.
2. One person picks up a card and, without looking at it, shows it to the other players.
3. The other players must describe the word on the card WITHOUT using the word itself.
4. The person holding the card must guess the word.
5. After guessing, talk about an instance where you experienced or used the social-emotional word on your card.
6. Repeat the game, with a different person picking a card each time.

Taking turns

Bullying

Excited

Sad

Angry

Listening

Body language

Boundaries

Kindness

Problem-solving

Rude

Trusting

Being helpful

Worried

Apologizing

Misunderstanding

Role-Play Fishbowl

You're about to go fishing—but not for fish! In this game, you're going to fish out different social situations and brainstorm the best way to handle them. Thinking through what you might do should you find yourself in these situations—or similar ones—can help you feel calmer and more prepared. Feel free to come up with a few situations of your own!

What You Need

- A bowl
- Pieces of paper, torn or cut into 2-by-2-inch squares
- Family and friends

Directions

1. Write numbers 1 through 10 on small pieces of paper, fold them up, and put them in a bowl.
2. Take turns picking a piece of paper. Find the situation that matches with your number, and read it aloud.
3. Talk with the group about what you would do (or have done!) to help you get through this situation.

Social Situations

1. Something embarrassing happened to you, and kids laughed

2. You beat your best friend at a game, and they are upset with you

3. A grown-up is making you do something you don't want to do

4. You received a gift you don't like

5. A stranger gave you a funny look

6. You are running late to school

7. Someone stands too close to you

8. Everyone in your friend group gets an invitation to a party except you

9. You accidentally reveal your friend's secret

10. A grown-up is angry at you for something you didn't do

Sharing Is Caring

Sharing is something both grown-ups and kids do all the time. We share our homes, toys, food, blankets, and many other things. Knowing that you can trust the friends you share with to give back your favorite toys is a great feeling. In this exercise, you're going to write down the things in your life that you are happy to share with someone and things that are just too difficult to share.

What You Need

- A grown-up

Directions

1. Using the worksheet, use your imagination to create a sharing agreement.
2. Work with a grown-up to think of different ways you can share even when it is tough.

Caregiver Tip: If your child struggles with sharing, talk to them before they play with friends about what toys they are willing to share with their friends. Encourage them to put special toys away to avoid sharing problems.

I, _____, agree that I will share _____

_____.

Sometimes when I share, I feel _____

_____.

I am not comfortable sharing _____.

If I am feeling upset about sharing, I can try _____

_____

or _____ to feel better about it.

Signature: _____

Draw some of your favorite things you would be willing to share with friends:

Respecting Others

Everyone is different. We all have unique feelings and ideas. But sometimes we have such strong feelings about something that it's hard to hear another person's opinion, especially when it's different from our own. But it's important to keep our ears and minds open to different ideas! In this exercise, you're going to practice how to respect an opinion that is different from yours.

What You Need

- A grown-up

Directions

1. What are some things that you have strong opinions about? This could be something such as your favorite superhero, your favorite sports team, or your favorite book or movie.
2. Use the T-chart to write 1 of your strong opinions at the top of the left column. Underneath, write down 3 to 5 reasons why you think your opinion is correct.
3. Now, have your grown-up write a differing opinion and their explanations on the right side.
4. Read your opinions out loud. Then the grown-up will read theirs.
5. When it's all done, think about how you felt hearing a different opinion from your own, and talk to your grown-up about it.

Caregiver Tip: You can use this activity with siblings to help them gain a better understanding of perspective-taking.

Social-Emotional Learning for Autistic Kids

Making Social Choices

Life is filled with making choices. What to eat for breakfast. What socks to wear. So. Many. Choices. Sometimes making a choice is easy, and other times it is not—especially when you're in a social situation that's making you a little nervous. When I'm in this kind of situation, it helps me to think about the choices I have and can make. I feel like I am in control! In this activity, you will practice making choices. Remember, there's no right or wrong answer, and the pros and cons will be different for different people.

What You Need

- A grown-up

Directions

1. Read the situation in the top box, then read the choice below. Read the pro and con of that choice.
2. Do you agree with the pro and con of this choice? Why or why not? Talk with a grown-up about your thoughts on the pro and con listed.
3. Now write down 2 other choices you could make in this situation, and come up with the pros and cons for each choice.
4. Talk with your grown-up about your choices and the pros and cons.

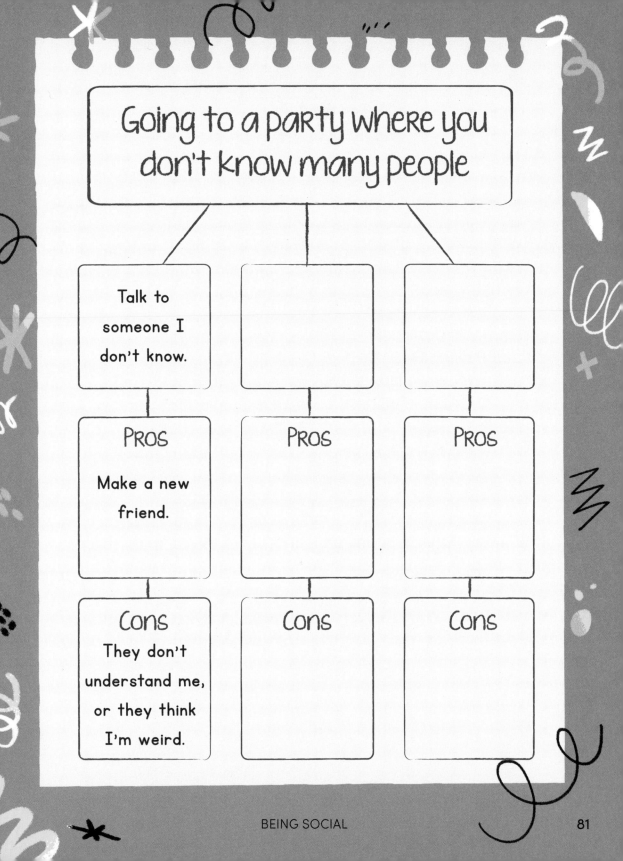

Going to a party where you don't know many people

Talk to someone I don't know.

PROS

Make a new friend.

Cons

They don't understand me, or they think I'm weird.

PROS

PROS

Cons

Cons

Chapter Wrap-Up

· ·

Figuring out social situations can sometimes feel like looking at a brand-new puzzle. There's a lot to figure out, but eventually you will put all the pieces together. Practice makes progress—as you interact with friends, family, and others around you, you'll get good at understanding and communicating with others. If you're ever anxious about being social, you can

- Make a plan using a choice chart like the one in **Making Social Choices** (page 80). Thinking through a scenario ahead of time can help you feel more confident when interacting with others in real life.

- Practice your social role-play skills, like you did in **Role-Play Fishbowl** (page 74). Ask a trusted grown-up to role-play a scenario that you're having difficulty with, so you can figure out the best way forward.

- Use a coping skill from Chapter 2, like an item from your **Coping Skills Toolbox** (page 42) or **Square Breathing** (page 40), to help you feel calmer.

CHAPTER 5

TALKING AND LISTENING TO OTHERS

It's time to learn the secrets of talking and listening like a pro. When you talk, it's like sending a message in a bottle, and when you listen, it's like finding that message! Communicating (that's a big word that means talking and listening) clearly and thoughtfully doesn't always come easy for a lot of people. The good news is that communication is a skill—you can learn and get better at it! In this chapter, you're going to complete activities that will help you

- practice listening and paying attention to what others have to say
- understand the importance of taking turns when you talk and listen
- discover ways to show others that you care about what they have to say
- learn how to ask questions to show that you are interested

Strengthening and growing your communication skills means that you will be able to build stronger relationships with others and express yourself in a clear and honest way!

Whole-Body Listening

Whole-body listening means using your senses to listen and pay attention to the person talking to you so that you can fully understand what's being said. For many people, that means their body is turned toward the person who is talking. Their hands and feet are still, their mouth is quiet, and they are looking at the speaker. But not everyone listens well this way! In this activity, you're going to consider how YOU use your whole body to listen in a way that makes you comfortable and allows you to hear what the speaker is saying.

What You Need

- A grown-up

Directions

1. Talk with a grown-up about how you like to listen and focus when someone is talking to you. What does your body do when you are listening?

2. Write down the different ways you use your whole body to listen.

Caregiver Tip: Not everyone is going to understand if your kid has a different listening style from what is expected. Talk with your kid about how they can advocate for themselves. For example, they might say that moving their hands or lowering their eyes actually helps them pay greater attention to what's being said.

When I'm listening...

my **eyes** are

my **mouth** is

my **body** is

my **legs and feet** are

my **hands** are

Get Ready to RACE

Being an active listener means paying attention when others talk to you. It is one way to show you care about someone, because you care about what they are telling you. In this exercise, you're going to learn the 4 steps of active listening. I call it being a RACE listener!

What You Need

- A grown-up

Directions

1. Look at what RACE stands for. Do you understand what each statement means? If not, ask a grown-up to explain!
2. Now, read the story and discuss the questions and your answers with a grown-up.

Receive the information.

Accept the information or instructions.

Consider your options to respond.

Engage or talk to the speaker.

It's a bright and sunny day in the park. A teacher, Ms. Rodriguez, is leading a lesson on birds, explaining to the students that they might see robins, sparrows, and finches. Ms. Rodriguez notes that they don't have enough binoculars for everyone in the class. Mia raises her hand and says, "Maybe we can pair up!" Ms. Rodriguez nods and smiles and thanks Mia for her good idea.

CONTINUED →

But not all the kids are paying attention. Alex and Sammie are chatting with each other, talking about Sammie's upcoming birthday party. Ms. Rodriguez notices and asks them if they can tell the class which bird they're most excited to see today. Alex looks ashamed and shakes his head no.

Sammie says that another student, Tommy, isn't paying attention because he is playing with a fidget toy. Tommy protests and says that he's most excited about finding a robin because he's never seen one before. Ms. Rodriguez gently reminds the class that everyone listens differently and that it can be great to have a fidget like Tommy's if they find it hard to concentrate and focus!

Discussion Questions

1. Who are the students using active listening skills during the lesson?
2. What part of RACE listening does Mia use?
3. How can Sammie and Alex use RACE listening to be better listeners?
4. How does Ms. Rodriguez know that Tommy has been listening?

Build-a-Scene

Play this fun game to practice taking turns—and your active listening skills! In this activity, you will take turns narrating and creating a scene. What listening skills will help you be successful?

What You Need

- A friend or family member

Directions

1. One person starts by saying a simple sentence or phrase, such as "The sky is blue."
2. The other person listens carefully and repeats the sentence, but adds another related sentence, like "The sky is blue. It's full of birds."
3. Take turns repeating phrases and adding on until you have a scene!
4. Talk about what happened as you were narrating the scene. Did either of you mishear or forget anything?
5. Repeating what is said can be a helpful listening skill! What other listening skills did you use? For example:
    - Did you wait for your partner to finish before speaking?
    - Did you face your partner as they were speaking?
6. Write down 2 more listening skills you used:

_____

_____

Storytelling and Storydrawing

Team up to create a story! When you work together, you can do a lot more than if you do it alone. In this exercise, one person will tell the other person a short story. The person who is listening has to draw the story. Remember to use your active listening skills here!

What You Need

- A friend or family member
- Paper
- Colored pencils or markers

Directions

1. Face each other and have your friend or family member tell you a short story.
2. As they tell you the story, begin to draw a general picture of what's happening in the story, but be sure to include important details!
3. When the storyteller is finished, have them write down their story on a piece of paper while you finish your drawing.
4. Compare their written story to your drawing. How well does your picture reflect what they said?
5. Feel free to get some more paper and do the activity again. This time, switch roles!

Activity Tip: Agree on a topic that you're both familiar with so you're not overwhelmed with drawing!

DRAW HERE:

Conversation Catch

Taking turns can be super hard to do, especially if you're waiting to do something exciting like riding a roller coaster. Even waiting for your turn to talk in class can be tricky. But when you're talking to someone, it's important to let them speak and not try to talk over them. It shows that you care about what they're telling you. In this exercise, you're going to play a game of catch to learn how to be a better listening partner and how to take turns talking.

What You Need

- 2 balls
- A friend or family member

Directions

1. To start, toss (or roll) a ball back and forth with your partner. Take notice of what you're doing so that you can be sure to catch the ball.
2. Now try turning away from your partner when they are throwing or rolling the ball.
3. Now take a second ball and toss it at the same time your partner is tossing their ball. Are you both able to catch the balls?
4. Complete the worksheet.

When were you most successful at catching the ball?

_____

_____

What happened when you turned away from your partner as they tried to throw you the ball?

_____

_____

What happened when the second ball was introduced?

_____

_____

How is throwing a ball back and forth with a partner like having a conversation with someone?

_____

_____

If you talk while the other person is talking, what might happen?

_____

_____

How do you feel when you are interrupted in a conversation?

_____

_____

Roll the Dice

Starting a conversation with someone you don't know can be scary. But talking with new people is how you start new friendships. This game will help you practice having conversations with people you know so you can feel more confident about starting a conversation with anyone. Switch up the game with your own questions!

What You Need

- A six-sided dice
- Friends and family

Directions

1. Take turns rolling the dice and answering the question that matches the number on the dice.
2. Now write 6 questions that you would want to ask a new friend!

Questions

1. Would you rather be able to fly or be invisible?
2. Is it better to have a fun friend or a kind friend?
3. What is the best gift you have ever received, and why is it special to you?
4. If you could have any animal for a pet, what would you choose?
5. What do you like most about school?
6. What's your favorite thing to do on the weekend?

1.

2.

3.

4.

5.

6.

Chapter Wrap-Up

Talking and listening are important for any relationship, whether it's with someone new or with family and friends we know well. They are key skills for effectively communicating with and understanding one another. When we talk, it's important to be clear and honest in our words. And when we listen, it's vital to pay attention and try to understand what the other person is saying. Here are some tips for brushing up your talking and listening skills:

- Show your teacher the **Storytelling and Storydrawing** activity (page 92), and ask them if you can lead the class in this activity.
- Revisit the listening skills you wrote down in **Build-a-Scene** (page 91) to remind yourself of your favorite ones. Jot down any new listening skills you've gained since you played the game!
- Come up with different questions for the **Roll the Dice** game (page 96), and play it with new friends.

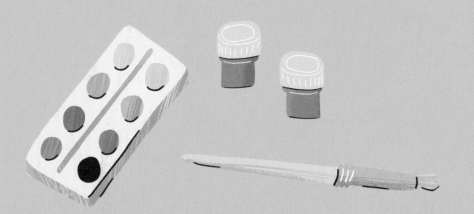

CHAPTER 6

JOINING IN AND MAKING FRIENDS

Making new friends is awesome. There's nothing like finding that person who laughs at the same jokes as you or who likes the same books, hobbies, and TV shows. Making new friends is such a wonderful feeling, but it does take a little bit of work. After you discover the people who you enjoy spending time with, make sure you treat them kindly so they'll want to remain your friend. In this chapter, you're going to learn about the different ways to make (and keep!) friends, including how to

- show interest in others by asking questions and listening actively to what they have to say
- share a little about yourself so other people can get to know you better
- be open to trying new things and meeting new people who share your interests
- solve conflicts and learn how to be a better, kinder friend

Remember to practice good communication skills, be respectful and considerate, and be patient, and you'll be making new friends in no time!

Friendship Cake

Friends come in all shapes and sizes, but there are some things about being a friend that are the same throughout any friendship. A good friend is kind, supportive, and respectful. They listen to you and are there for you when you need help or want to talk. They're honest and accept you for who you are. In this activity, you're going to make a friendship cake—on paper—that has all the ingredients you think are important to being a good friend.

What You Need

- Colored pencils or markers
- Stickers (optional)
- A grown-up

Directions

1. Color and decorate the blank friendship cake using colored pencils, markers, or stickers.
2. Fill in the blanks to create a recipe for your friendship cake.
3. Talk through your friendship choices with a grown-up and ask them what they would put in their friendship cake.

Caregiver Tip: When you finish this activity with your child, make a real cake together. Use the different ingredients as a fun way to help your kid remember the key components of making and maintaining friendships. For example, you can use the sugar to represent kindness, the flour to represent stability and honesty, and the eggs to represent flexibility and open-mindedness.

Social-Emotional Learning for Autistic Kids

Ingredients for a Friendship Cake:

A spoonful of ___Honesty_____

2 dashes of _____

A pinch of _____

A squeeze of _____

2 cups of _____

½ cup of _____

Being a Good Friend

Being a good friend is a big responsibility. It involves a lot of different feelings, emotions, and even commitments. The great thing about being a good friend is when you find that person you want to be around. You want to share your thoughts and feelings with them and hear about what they think and feel. In this exercise, you're going to read a short story that explores the ideas of what it means to be a good friend and what it means to not be a good friend.

What You Need

- A grown-up

Directions

1. Read the short story.
2. Read the questions, and discuss your answers with a grown-up.

Caregiver Tip: Encourage your child to talk to you about their friendships and how they are feeling. This can help you understand your child's perspective. Offer support and guidance if they are having a difficult time with a friend.

Jake was playing basketball with his school friends and his neighbor, Sam, at the park. Sam was having a hard time keeping up with the game and kept making mistakes. Jake started to get frustrated and annoyed with Sam, so he loudly complained about Sam to the other kids and made fun of Sam's mistakes. This made Sam feel embarrassed, and he stopped wanting to play.

1. How was Jake not being a good friend to Sam?
2. Was there anything Sam could do to get Jake to stop teasing him?
3. How would you have helped Sam if you were playing basketball with them?
4. What would you say to Jake to get him to stop teasing Sam?
5. What would you say to Sam to make him feel better about playing basketball?

Would You Rather?

Becoming friends with someone means you get to learn all kinds of interesting things about them. Would You Rather? is a fun and easy game you can play with friends—new and old—to get to know them better. And you can even come up with your own questions together!

What You Need

- Friend or family member

Directions

1. Take turns asking the Would You Rather? questions.
2. Talk about your answers and why you chose them.

Caregiver Tip: Would You Rather? is a great way to give your child a choice when you need them to do something that might be challenging for them. For example, you might say, "It's time for bed! Would you rather put on your pajamas first or brush your teeth first?"

Would you rather be a
scuba diver or an **astronaut**?

Would you rather live in
a **city** or in the **country**?

Would you rather win
a **lifetime supply of candy** or
a **lifetime pass to an**
amusement park?

Would you rather
stay up late or **get up early**?

Would you rather visit a
new country every year or
get an **expensive new toy**
every year?

Old Friends, New Experiences

Throughout your life, you will have many chances to try new things: new games to play, new foods to eat, new places to go. Sometimes people get scared or anxious about trying something new, which is natural. In this exercise, you're going to think of something new you want to try with a friend and use the circle to help you break it down into smaller steps so it's less scary.

What You Need

- A grown-up

Directions

1. Think of a new activity that you and a friend want to try together. For example, learning to play a new game or taking a new class.
2. Write down that activity in the middle of the circle.
3. Brainstorm with a grown-up the different steps you might need to take to do this new activity with your friend. For example, think about what you might need to bring with you, what clothing or equipment you might need, or what you might ask for help with.
4. Write these steps down in the wedges of the chart, from 1 to 7. (You might not need all 7 steps.)
5. Now, go ahead and follow the plan!

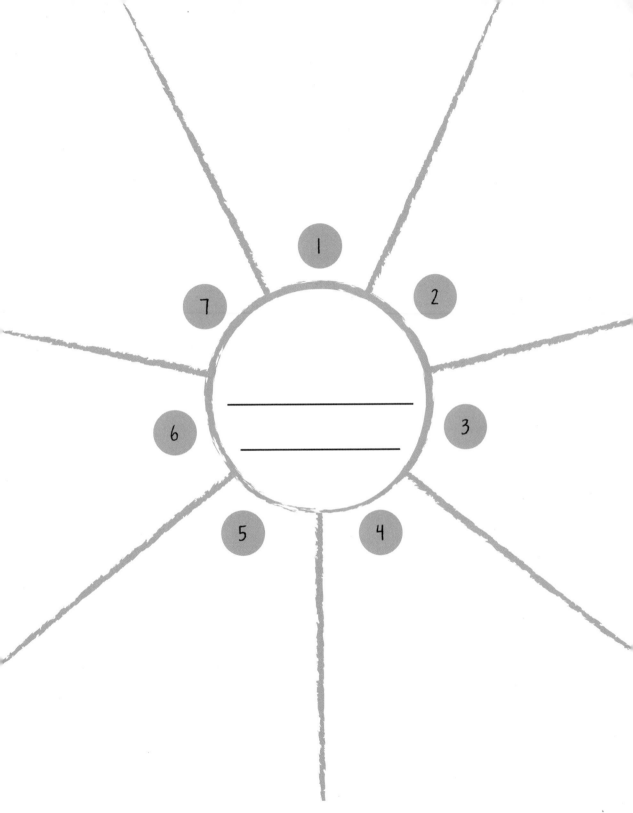

Ticket to Friendship Story

Imagine that you're taking a trip to Hawaii with a friend, but you have different ideas about what you want to do when you get there. You're going to need to compromise if you both want to have a fun time on vacation. This means finding a solution that works for both of you. Like choosing something different that both of you can agree on, or taking turns being the decision-maker. In this exercise, you will write a story about compromise by filling in the blanks. There are no right or wrong answers!

Directions

1. Read the story on pages 111–112.
2. Fill in the blanks with compromises you might make on a trip with your friend.

Caregiver Tip: Model compromise in your own interactions. For example, if you are trying to decide on a snack to have together, you could say something like "I really want a piece of fruit, but you want a cookie. How about we have a piece of fruit now and save a cookie for later?" This helps the child see how compromise works in practice.

My friend _____ and I

are so excited about our trip to Hawaii! On the plane, we

got into an argument because I was most excited about

doing _____

_____

first, but my friend wanted to try _____

_____

_____ first.

Our parents suggested we compromise by _____

_____

_____

_____.

    While at the beach, our parents asked if we wanted

to try snorkeling. I said no, but my friend said yes. We

decided that a good compromise would be to _____

_____.

CONTINUED ➔

That night we were both super hungry and we both wanted to go out for dinner. I really wanted to eat _____ _____, but my friend wanted to eat _____ _____. We decided to compromise (again) by

_____

_____

_____.

Social-Emotional Learning for Autistic Kids

Finding Solutions

Friendships and conflicts are a normal part of life. In this exercise, you're going to read a story about a disagreement among three friends and offer some solutions to help them resolve the problem.

Directions

1. Read the short story.
2. Answer the questions. Discuss them with a grown-up, if you'd like.

. . . .

Sara, Ben, and Katie were playing a game of tag at the park. They were having a great time, but then Ben accidentally tripped and fell and hurt his ankle. Sara and Katie rushed over to see if he was okay. They knew they needed to get him help, but neither wanted to go home to get a grown-up. That's because they were playing in a park they were not allowed to go to. It was far from their neighborhood, and their parents didn't want them going there after school.

Katie thought Sara should run home because it was her idea to play at that park. Sara thought Katie should run home because she lived closer to Ben's family. They went back and forth for a few minutes with no solution. Both girls refused to

CONTINUED ➜

budge. Ben sat on the ground, looking more and more upset. Finally, he shouted, "Hey! Can you just stop arguing and help me? My ankle really hurts, and I'm scared."

Sara felt bad, and she finally agreed to run to get help because it was her idea to play at that park. She got her parents to drive her back, and they also called Ben's and Katie's parents. Ben ended up being okay, but everyone was grounded for a few days because they had broken their parents' rules.

Questions

1. What caused the conflict in the story? How did the friends react to it?

_____

_____

2. How did the friends try to resolve the conflict? Were their methods effective? Why or why not?

_____

_____

3. What could the friends have done differently to prevent or resolve the conflict?

_____

_____

4. What do you think the friends learned from the experience? How do you think it changed their friendship?

_____

_____

Chapter Wrap-Up

You've learned all about making new friends and practiced all sorts of skills that go into building strong, healthy relationships with others, like learning to compromise, understanding what goes into a good friendship, and learning how to be a better friend. All these skills will help you build friendships that are based on trust, respect, and mutual understanding. If you need help navigating friendships, you can try:

- Playing a fun game together, like **Would You Rather?** (p. 106) or **Roll the Dice** from Chapter 5 (page 96). That can help break the ice between new friends, and help you get to know good friends even better.
- Revisiting your **Friendship Cake** recipe (page 102) to remind yourself what ingredients you need to have a good friendship.
- Remembering the skills you worked on in other chapters that can help you solve friendship conflicts, like how to communicate your feelings (Chapter 3) and how to be a good listener (Chapter 5).

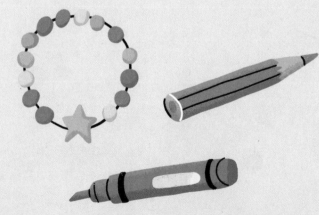

CHAPTER 7

RESPECTING BOUNDARIES

We've talked a little bit about boundaries and respect in other parts of this book. Now we are going to dig a little deeper into the topic. Boundaries are the limits we set for ourselves and others. For example, a boundary might be that you always decline invitations to big birthday parties at the local park because the noise of a lot of kids running around is overwhelming for you. Respect is about showing consideration and understanding for someone's boundaries. An example of respecting a boundary is knowing that your friend doesn't want you playing with their action figures without asking, so you always remember to ask before you play with them at their house. In this chapter, you will learn

- how to figure out your own boundaries
- how to make sure people respect your boundaries
- how to maintain your personal space and respect others' personal space
- how to handle misunderstandings or miscommunications around boundaries and consent

Boundary Circles

There are a lot of different people in your life, and what boundaries you have for them—meaning what you choose to do or share with them—depends a lot on how close and comfortable you feel around them. This activity is about figuring out which people in your life are the closest to you, which are not, and which are somewhere in between.

Directions

1. Think about the people who you are closest to, and write their names in circle 1. These people could be your parents, other family members, or best friends.
2. Now, think about other people who you may see often but aren't super close to, such as a teacher or a class friend. Write them down in circle 2.
3. In circle 3, write down the names of people you don't know well at all, such as a neighbor, a distant family member, or your mail carrier.
4. On page 122, write down or draw one thing you'd be comfortable doing with the people in each circle and one thing you wouldn't. For example, you might be comfortable hugging those in your inner circle, but not those in the outermost circle.

Caregiver Tip: Continue to have conversations with your child about their boundary circles. You can also try setting up physical boundaries using cones or Hula-Hoops while you have this discussion. Sometimes using a concrete visual example can help autistic kids who struggle with abstract concepts better understand the idea.

3

2

1

You

CONTINUED →

- Circle 1:

- Circle 2:

- Circle 3:

Personal Space

Personal space is a, well, very personal thing. Personal space is all about how close you want someone to you or how close you can be to someone. For example, you might be okay sitting next to someone you know well (think parents, siblings, best friends) but not someone you don't know well (like a stranger on the bus). Sometimes, it's easy to know when a friend needs some personal space—maybe they will just tell you or maybe you know by looking at their face. Other times, it can feel hard to ask a friend to leave you alone, because you don't want to hurt their feelings. For this activity, we're going to travel to space to practice our personal space skills.

Directions

Read the prompts on pages 124–125 and answer the questions.

Caregiver Tip: It can be very hard for autistic kids to ask for space and to accept when others tell them that they need space. If this exercise makes them feel upset, remind them of the Square Breathing technique they learned in Chapter 2 (page 40). Even just taking a few deep breaths (do it with them!) can help them regulate their emotions.

CONTINUED ➔

How can you tell when a friend might need some personal space?

How do you feel when a friend tells you they need more space?

Social-Emotional Learning for Autistic Kids

How do you feel when you don't have enough space?

What is one way you can tell someone that you need space?

STOP!

Part of learning about your boundaries is also learning how to let someone know when their actions or words make you feel angry, uncomfortable, or sad. For this activity, you're going to come up with 3 ways to respectfully say no. Remember, this doesn't mean you have to yell! You can tell someone in a calm way without raising your voice that you don't like what they are doing.

What You Need

- A grown-up

Directions

1. Brainstorm with your grown-up ways to respectfully say no or "stop." For example, you might say, "No, thank you. I don't want to do that" or "I've changed my mind. Please stop."
2. Write down 3 different answers, and practice saying the words out loud.

Caregiver Tip: Hearing and accepting the word no can be just as difficult as saying no. One way to get kids to understand that no means no is to ask them to think about how it makes them feel when they ask someone to stop and are ignored.

1.
_____

_____

2.
_____

_____

3.
_____

_____

A Line in the Sand

Have you heard the phrase "drawing a line in the sand"? Grown-ups say this a lot! It's another way of talking about boundaries and the kinds of activities and situations you are willing to participate in—and those you are not. In this activity, you're going to read about different types of activities and decide if they sound like things you would want to do or not.

Directions

1. Read each scenario.
2. Circle YES if you would like to participate or NO if you would not.
3. Think about what the NO scenarios have in common and what the YES scenarios have in common. What does that tell you about your boundaries?
4. Also consider what might change to turn your NO into a YES and a YES into a NO. For example, if you said NO to a classmate borrowing your favorite toy, would you say YES if it were a sibling or close friend?

Activity Tip: Turn this into a sensory activity! Build a sand tray with figurines and sand toys or tools, and discuss each scenario with a grown-up while using your tools to create lines or other boundaries around the figurines.

1. A friend wants to play a game that involves chasing each other. YES NO

2. A classmate asks if they can borrow your favorite stuffie. YES NO

3. A family member asks if you want to go on a hike with them. YES NO

4. A friend asks if you want to have a sleepover. YES NO

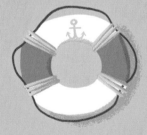

5. A family member asks if you will give them a hug. YES NO

Flexible or Not?

Some rules you have for yourself may not change, such as never cross the street on a red light. Others may change as you learn and grow. For example, as you get older, you may feel more comfortable with people borrowing your stuff. For this exercise, you're going to use cooked and uncooked noodles to figure out the differences between rules that can be HARD and those that can be FLEXIBLE. Ask a grown-up to prepare the noodles for you before you start this activity.

What You Need

- Cooked noodles
- Uncooked noodles
- 2 empty containers
- A grown-up

Directions

1. Read each rule. If you think the rule is flexible, put a cooked noodle in a container. If you think the rule is not flexible, put an uncooked noodle in the other container.
2. Use the blank lines to write out other rules that you follow, and see if they are HARD or might be FLEXIBLE in the future.
3. Discuss your answers with a grown-up, and see if they agree with you.

Caregiver Tip: If your child does not like the sensory feeling of a cooked noodle, you can use pipe cleaners instead.

Rules

- "Beware of Dog."
- Your bedtime is at 8:00 p.m.
- "Keep Out!"
- Tablet time is after you finish your homework.
- You must eat all your vegetables at dinner.
- You have to return a book on time to the library.
- No sweets on weekdays.
- Your choice:

_____

_____

- Your choice:

_____

_____

- Your choice:

_____

_____

Bubble Trouble

Everyone has an invisible bubble around them. This bubble is our personal space. Play this fun game with friends or family to better understand the concept of personal space!

What You Need

- Cones, or something to mark the ground
- Hula-Hoop
- Friends or family

Directions

1. Find an open space. If possible, choose a spot outdoors with plenty of room to move.
2. Place the cones or markers in a random pattern on the ground, at least 2 feet apart.
3. Give a Hula-Hoop to each player, and have them each stand at a cone.
4. When you say "go," each player should hold their Hula-Hoops around their waist and run between the cones. Try to avoid each other as you run!
5. Did you bump into anyone? How did they react? Did anyone bump into you? How did that make you feel?

Caregiver Tip: If your child has trouble keeping personal space during the game, put the Hula-Hoop on the ground and see if they can keep their body inside for 30 seconds. Or try sharing their Hula-Hoop for a little bit, and talk about what it felt like to have less space.

Chapter Wrap-Up

Learning about boundaries is so important because it helps you build healthy and respectful relationships. By understanding and respecting others' boundaries, you show that you care about their feelings and needs. Just like any other skill, practice makes progress. Keep working on respecting boundaries by:

- Asking your teacher if your whole class can play **Bubble Trouble** (page 132) so everyone can learn about personal space.
- Revisiting your **Boundary Circles** (page 120) and using it to remind yourself of what you're comfortable with and what you're not. Has anything changed since you first filled it in?
- Playing the **Flexible or Not?** game (page 130) in your head when you encounter a new boundary or a new rule someone has given you. But remember to ask the person who gave you that boundary, to see if you've understood them correctly!
- Reminding yourself of the respectful ways you came up with to say no in **STOP!** (page 126).

CHAPTER 8

HANDLING THE HARD STUFF

Life has many ups and downs. Sometimes it may seem like there are more downs than ups. Maybe at school you dropped your morning snack on the ground, and in the afternoon you got into an argument with a classmate over a book. When nothing seems to be going right, it can be hard to not feel sad and mad. You may even want to give up and go home. But learning to handle all the hard stuff that comes your way is a gift. This skill is called *resilience*, and it means that even though something didn't go the way you hoped, you are able to cope with the disappointment and continue being your best self. In this chapter, we'll learn

- how to handle things when they don't go the way you wanted or expected
- more techniques to cool our emotions
- effective ways to say sorry and correct our mistakes
- how to advocate for yourself

These skills are super important—especially as you get older, when you're an adult out in the world.

Bumps in the Road

Pretend it's a beautiful day, and you are going to the park with a friend. Both of you are excited to try your new skateboard. But as soon as you get on and start the course, you hit a rock and fall off. It's natural to feel upset and want to stop. But learning to get up and keep going is an important skill. In this exercise, you're going to come up with ways to help yourself overcome obstacles and make it through the course.

What You Need

- A grown-up

Directions

1. Read each scenario, and think about how you might feel and what you would do to overcome this obstacle.
2. Write down your responses and discuss them with a grown-up.

Caregiver Tip: Talk with your child about your own "bumps" in the road. Let them know about some of the obstacles you've overcome as a child and as an adult.

You did something wrong
and got in trouble.

_____
_____

Your friend was mean to you,
and you do not know why.

_____
_____

Your friend broke something
special that belongs to you.

_____
_____

You are starting a new school.

_____
_____

Cool-Down Cards

Remembering how to stay calm in difficult situations is not an easy thing to do. We've already learned a few self-calming skills in Chapter 2, and now we're going to learn a few more. Let's make some Cool-Down Cards so you remember how to "cool down" when you're feeling overwhelmed or frustrated!

What You Need

- Colored pencils or markers
- Index cards
- Stickers (optional)
- Binder clip

Directions

1. Read the sample Cool-Down Cards, and if you like those ideas, write them down on your own cards.
2. Come up with some of your own cool-down ideas, and write them on your cards. Brainstorm with a grown-up, if you want.
3. Color and decorate your cards with drawings or stickers to remind you of each coping skill.
4. Use a binder clip to organize your cards. Remember to carry them with you!

Caregiver Tip: Make your own Cool-Down Cards with your kids, and model how to use them. Seeing you use your cards to calm down before reacting or escalating will help them remember to use theirs.

1. Breathe into your belly.

2. Say something positive about yourself out loud.

3. Picture a quiet and happy place.

4. Count to 10 with your eyes closed.

Online Safety

Finding fun things to do online is wonderful. It can be a fun way to talk and play with friends. Maybe you get to talk to a grandparent or family member from far away. Perhaps you use the Internet to do homework or play a video game. All of these online activities are cool, but the Internet can also be a dangerous place, so it comes with special rules. In this activity, you're going to practice rules to follow when you are online. Make sure you do this with a grown-up so you can check in with them about your answers.

What You Need

- A grown-up

Directions

1. Read each scenario.
2. Discuss your answers with the grown-up.

Caregiver Tip: It's important to set clear guidelines for your kiddo's Internet use and educate them about the potential dangers of the Internet. Use parental controls, and discuss privacy settings with them to protect their personal information. The parents' guidebooks at ConnectSafely (connectsafely.org) are a great resource to help you with this.

I'm online, and I meet someone my age in a game chat room. Is it okay to give them my address or phone number so we can get together in person?

I have a picture of myself on my tablet, and someone I met online wants to see it. Is it okay to send it to that person?

I'm visiting a website from a store that I've heard of. They want my name and phone number so I can enter a contest. Is it okay to enter?

My parents and I have established rules as to what I can do on the Internet when I'm home, but I'm at a friend's house. Should I go by my parents' rules or do whatever my friend does?

What's Behind Your Mask?

Sometimes we try to hide certain things about ourselves from others because we are afraid they won't like us. But being true to yourself is one of the kindest things you can do. When you try to hide who you are, it can make you feel very tired and sad. It can even make it harder for you to make true friends. It's important for people to understand and accept that autism is just a part of who you are and a part of what makes you, *you.*

Directions

1. In the mask, write down some things you feel like you need to hide from people. Maybe you don't want your friends to know you use fidgets, or maybe you pretend to like something that your friends do, because you don't want to feel left out.
2. In the sign, write ways to share that information. For example, explain how the fidgets are helpful so you can focus and learn all the information in school.

Caregiver Tip: Pair this activity with Boundary Circles (page 120) or What's Your Hidden Treasure? (page 61), and encourage your kid to think about the difference between not being ashamed of their unique personality, needs, or behaviors and sharing information with people they might regret.

Things You Should Know about Me

Self-advocacy is the ability to speak up for yourself. It's about making sure that what you need and want is expressed. Maybe you like to sit to the left of your teacher when they read stories to the class. Learning to explain your different likes and dislikes is important because it helps you understand yourself better. And when you understand yourself better, you are more confident in making decisions!

What You Need

- A grown-up

Directions

1. Think about times when you needed to let a grown-up know something about yourself but were scared.
2. In the magnifying glass, write 3 things you might be worried about letting someone know.
3. Talk with a grown-up about some ways to make it easier for you to tell others about your needs.

Activity Tip: When speaking up for yourself, use a calm and respectful tone. Use assertive body language, such as making eye contact if you can and standing up straight, to show that you are confident. When others are speaking, you can practice active listening (see Chapter 5) by paying attention and asking clarifying questions.

_____

_____

_____

_____

_____

_____

_____

_____

Sadness Rock

When you feel sad, how does it feel in your body? Maybe your chest feels heavy? Or you just want to curl up in bed? Sadness is a common emotion everyone experiences and one that we all need to learn to process so that it doesn't overwhelm us. One of the best ways to process your sadness is to get creative. For this exercise, you are going to paint a rock that expresses how you feel when you're sad. You're using a rock because they are heavy, just like sometimes your feelings can be heavy, too.

What You Need

- A medium-size smooth rock
- A grown-up
- Paint or paint pens

Directions

1. Hold the rock and think about the colors that show what sadness feels like to you.
2. Paint your rock in a way that represents something that feels sad or difficult in your life. Use words, drawings, or both—whatever feels right to you.
3. Talk about your rock, what it represents, and why you're feeling sad with a grown-up.
4. There's no rush, but when you feel ready, you can hide your rock or even get rid of it to represent that you are letting go of your sadness or saying goodbye to that challenging moment.

Caregiver Tip: Make a sadness rock with your child to normalize their feelings. Discuss what the rock represents and how you helped yourself overcome a difficult or sad time in your life.

Saying Sorry

Saying sorry is an important way to show that you care about other people's feelings and that you take responsibility for your actions. When you do something that hurts someone else, it's important to apologize and try to make things right. But saying sorry can be really, really hard to do. Even though it shows you are brave and that you want to fix things, apologizing doesn't come easy for many, many people. In this exercise, you're going to learn how to become a pro at saying sorry.

What You Need

- A grown-up
- A book that you own or have checked out from the library where a character makes a mistake. If you can't think of one, here are some options for you:
  - Natasha Yim, *Goldy Luck and the Three Pandas*
  - Rukhsana Khan, *Big Red Lollipop*
  - Marcy Campbell, *Adrian Simcox Does NOT Have a Horse*

Directions

1. Read your book with a grown-up.
2. Talk about the story and who was wrong. Did they make things better? How? Were they forgiven?
3. Now answer the questions on the next page and discuss them with a grown-up.

Social-Emotional Learning for Autistic Kids

1. Name a time when you did something wrong and found it hard to say sorry.

_____

_____

2. Why did you find it hard?

_____

_____

_____

3. How did the situation end?

_____

_____

_____

4. What do you wish you did differently? How could you do better next time?

_____

_____

_____

_____

Chapter Wrap-Up

You've learned some great strategies for coping with challenges and setbacks and for dealing with difficult emotions. You know how to express yourself in healthy ways, bounce back from failure, and keep going even when things get tough. These skills will help you become stronger and more resilient and will serve you well in all areas of life. If life ever feels too overwhelming or hard, try:

- Expressing yourself creatively to help you process a heavy emotion, like you did in **Sadness Rock** (page 146).
- Reflecting on your solutions in **What's Behind Your Mask?** (page 142) and **Things You Should Know about Me** (page 144) to remind you of the ways you can speak up for yourself.
- Practicing your favorite coping skills from your **Cool-Down Cards** (page 138) every day, especially when you feel calm, so you'll be ready to use them when you're not feeling calm.

You're Doing Great!

Congratulations on taking the time to learn about yourself and to practice these awesome social and emotional skills! I know this book was a lot of work, but now that you're finished, you have many great new tools to help you at school and home. Here are some of the social and emotional skills you practiced in this book:

- Recognizing and expressing your thoughts, feelings, and needs
- Managing your emotions and calming your body down when needed
- Building and maintaining healthy relationships
- Communicating effectively with others
- Navigating social situations and social cues
- Handling tough situations and challenges in life

Keep practicing these skills. Don't be afraid to make mistakes; this is how we grow and learn. Keep striving to be the best version of yourself, and remember that it's okay to ask for help when you need it.

You've got this!

Resources

Autistic Self Advocacy Network (ASAN)

autisticadvocacy.org

ASAN is a national grassroots disability rights organization run by and for autistic people. They provide resources, support, and advocacy for the autism community.

Camouflage: The Hidden Lives of Autistic Women **by Dr. Sarah Bargiela**

An illustrated book that offers insight into the lives and minds of autistic women based on real-life stories and case studies.

The Reason I Jump: The Inner Voice of a Thirteen-Year-Old Boy with Autism **by Naoki Higashida**

This book, written by a young autistic boy, provides insight into his thoughts and life experiences as an autistic individual.

The Girl Who Thought in Pictures: The Story of Dr. Temple Grandin **by Julia Finley Mosca**

This picture book tells the story of Temple Grandin, a famous autistic scientist and advocate. It provides a positive and inspiring message for young autistic children.

CONTINUED →

***The Incredible 5-Point Scale* by Kari Dunn Buron and Mitzi Curtis**

This book teaches autistic kids how to use a 5-point scale to understand and regulate their emotions. It includes strategies for managing challenging behaviors and building self-awareness.

***The Autism Acceptance Book* by Ellen Sabin**

This book, written specifically for autistic kids, promotes self-acceptance and understanding of neurodiversity.

Neurodivergent Rebel podcast

neurodivergentrebel.com/category/podcasts

This podcast features interviews with neurodivergent individuals and their allies, discussing issues related to neurodiversity and disability rights.

ACTIVITIES BY SUBJECT

ACTIVITIES BY MODALITY

Acknowledgments

I am deeply grateful to the many individuals who supported me throughout the writing of this book.

First and foremost, I would like to thank my husband, sister, and parents for their unwavering encouragement and belief in my abilities. Their guidance and support were invaluable to me as I navigated the challenges of writing a book.

I would also like to express my gratitude to my friends Jennah, Randi, Brittany, Jill, and Kelsey for their invaluable feedback and edits. Their insights and suggestions helped to shape the final product and make it the best it could be.

Finally, I am thankful for the rest of my family and friends who provided love and support throughout the writing process. Their patience and understanding allowed me to fully focus on the task at hand and bring this book to fruition.

I am forever grateful for the support and encouragement of these individuals, and I could not have completed this project without them.

About the Author

Emily Mori, MS, LCPC, CAS, is a certified strength-based therapist and autism specialist. She has a master's degree in clinical mental health counseling from Johns Hopkins University and a bachelor's degree in psychology and sociology from Lebanon Valley College. Emily has extensive experience working with individuals with developmental disabilities and is a certified ADHD clinical services provider. In her work with children, adolescents, and young adults, Emily helps clients navigate challenges with academics, parenting, family dynamics, and other issues. She is passionate about working with autistic individuals and helping them navigate transitional periods. Emily's goal is to empower her clients and help them find practical, long-term solutions to their problems.

About the Illustrator

Victoria Stebleva is an internationally published illustrator currently living in Nish, Serbia. The variety of her work is quite large, from illustrations for children's books to editorial illustrations on socially important topics for media. Victoria is fond of motorbike traveling, nonfiction literature, rock music, and cats. Parents, for more information on Victoria's illustrations, follow her on Instagram @vika_stebleva.

Hi, parents and caregivers,

We hope *Social-Emotional Learning for Autistic Kids* helped you and your child. If you have any questions or concerns about your book, or have received a damaged copy, please contact customerservice@penguinrandomhouse.com. We're here and happy to help.

Also, please consider writing a review on your favorite retailer's website to let others know what you thought of the book.

Sincerely,
The Zeitgeist Team